DEEP DIVE

DEEP DIVE

Deep Dive

Karen Carter

QUERENCIA
Querencia Press
Chicago IL

QUERENCIA PRESS

© Copyright 2024
Karen Carter

All Rights Reserved

No reproduction, copy or transmission of this publication may be
made without written permission.
No paragraph of this publication may be reproduced, copied or
transmitted save with the written permission of the author.

Any person who commits any unauthorized act in relation to this
publication may be liable to criminal prosecution and civil claims
for damages.

ISBN 978 1 963943 10 8

Unaltered cover photo "Moorland Landscape" by Charlotte Christie
Digitally manipulated by Emily Perkovich

www.querenciapress.com

First Published in 2024

Querencia Press, LLC
Chicago IL

Printed & Bound in the United States of America

ADVANCE PRAISE FOR DEEP DIVE

"Karen Carter takes the path that so many poets have followed to contemplate what their lives have meant, not only for themselves but also for a poesy of love and forgiveness. In *Deep Dive*, her first book of poetry, Karen looks back at her life—through eloquence, beauty, truth, and pain—to finally accept the reality of her estrangement from herself. In twenty-four poems, she replays her life story, beginning with her childhood trauma, and in her later years, bridges the path of enlightenment and self-awareness. For her, *Deep Dive* is a mindful poetic presence, as she writes in the poem, "Back to the Roots": "I no longer need / a mustard seed to grow./ My interior tells me / the time has come to shed the exterior, / like the full-blown tree knows / it must give up its centerpiece / cornucopia, its fruits and flowers, / so that the tree returns to its roots." Such is the gift of Karen's deep dive just as her epiphany is to lifelong revelation."

—Sandra Fluck, Editor, The Write Launch

"From the therapy chairs of Oklahoma to the solitude of her front porch in rural North Carolina; from the classroom during COVID to the beaches of the Outer Banks, Karen Carter asks us to dive deep into the natural world and dive even deeper into our suffering, courage and healing. She interrogates a dragonfly: "My dear dragonfly, what do your eyes see?" She faces her nightmares and flashbacks of the violence done to her body and mind. With great courage, she chooses to dig her feet into the sand and, like Jesus, drive the demonic pigs into the sea. Finally, she releases her "sobs without shame to the Begotten, not Made, while the waves roll on into eternity."

If your heart wants a companion as it dives deep into the grief and ashes of life where at the bottom of the dive there is healing and hope and newness of life to be found, then this book will become your treasured friend, a candle when the night wind blows."

—(Rev) Curtis M. Abbott, D.Min, LPC, LMFT. Co-Founder of The Center for Psychotherapy, Education and Spiritual Growth, Inc. in Oklahoma City.

To Curtis

My Shepherd and My Shrink

CONTENTS

Introduction 11

Talking Trees 15
In the Spirit of Emily Dickinson 17
Wear a White Rose 18
When fear rises 20
Deposited Deep 22
One Brief Moment 23
Where a Turtle Leads 25
Veins 26
Page Torn from Tea Leaves 27
Between Being and Doing 28
November Cloak 29
Turn Signals 31
Thanksgiving 33
Nameless Tumbleweeds 34
Sacred Land 35
Winter Breath 36
Slate Blue 38
Awakened 40
(Red Tulips) 40
Kick the Can 43
The Unfettered Life 45
Forgiven 47
Ladybug Blues 48
Citrus Delight 52
Front Porch Sitting 53
Solitude 55

The Great Monarch Migration 57
Dragonfly 59
Hope seals the virus 62
Desolate 65
First Bells 67
Time Capsule 69
Back to the Roots 71
The Bridge 73
Rise Up Geranium Word-Gems 74
(Pelargoniums) 74
Painting Words 76
A Forecast of Severe Storms Today 78
Lullaby 80
Ocean Surfing 82
Body Splash 84
To the Begotten, not Made 85
Sent into the Sea 88
Coquina Beach 90
Harboring Hope 93

Acknowledgements 99

Introduction

I sat on my front porch in spring 2020. Globally, we all know the season: shutdown COVID-19. At that time, I taught in public school and lived in Tyrrell County, a rural-remote area an hour's drive from the Outer Banks, North Carolina. With high school remote in March 2020, my front porch was my sanctuary. My companions were creatures of nature: the birdsong a constant solace, the flutter of the butterflies in the azalea bush, and even the lizards that checked in on me while I checked them out ("Front Porch Sitting"). Black bear plopped down on the wheat field. A little cub danced around the light pole in my backyard. Red Fox poked their heads out of the corn patch. A Great Horned Owl perched on my backyard clothesline and flew to sit right in front of me on my front porch. A dragonfly rested on my teacup and sometimes my toes while we relaxed—I in my beach chair—with a book and a writing journal.

Poetry poured out of me on paper, like "ripping those veins right out of my skin" ("Veins"). I had no real desire to publish poetry. I just needed to make sense of it all—or to be more honest—"sit with sorrow" ("To the Begotten, Not Made"). Writing grounded me like the "pen waits to grasp the common word" ("Between Being and Doing"). I knew I had to write. I had a story to tell, a memoir in poetry.

In those pandemic years, the dragonfly gave me vision. Never let up. I struggled to know whether to return to public school—now hybrid. My big head attached to my little neck hurt, but I found the courage to click on the teacher's online survey: "I'm not a robot." I'm legit; I'm in. I returned to school even though I was closing in on 70 years of age ("Dragonfly").

My front porch sitting and writing poetry did not stop. My well was overflowing with water, trees, plants, and flowers and more creatures of nature giving imagery to my voice ("Rise Up Geranium Word-Gems"). In the front yard, I watched a Northern Cardinal, masked up with its little red coat on, dip for food. I absorbed droplets of hope, writing about the injured bird getting well from the care of a nurse ("Hope seals the virus").

I was the wounded cardinal, and it was time to write about my breakdown, in hope that my poetry might be moving and healing to those who have had to live in and come from "hell back," "like a prison of seaweed twisted and torn with a rancor odor not even bathing could cleanse" ("To the Begotten, Not Made"). As early as Fall 2020, I shared my poems with an audience through publication. I was fortunate these nature images connected with people that read them. I kept teaching and writing and getting published. I returned to revising poems I had written when I taught and lived and broke down in Oklahoma City. At age 35, I had stood on the steps of a university and asked a psychotherapist for help.

The breakdown was long and hard, and "my smudged-over lies" from shame and psychotic guilt made my "longing of a constant tree" with early on-set depression severe. The medical prognosis was not good, even to the point that perhaps long-term institutionalization with heavy drugs might be the best that could be done. But nearly 40 years later and with therapy since 1987, "the tree pruned from brittle branches" is "no longer distanced from the wind breathing mass into the rib" ("Page Torn from Tea Leaves"). This poem, my first published poem, the year 2003, tells where I have come from.

All these years and especially from 2020 to 2023, each day sitting on my front porch, I stayed in the present, the fog serving as a moving map, a guide when fear rises early in the morning ("When fear rises"). School was back in-person with some hybrid class settings from quarantines, and the ocean was an hour's drive away.

Summer 2022, it was time to visit the ocean. For two to three days every week that summer, I heard the waves sing their lullaby of surrender to me ("Lullaby"). Ocean sounds "released my sobs without shame" and my ocean poems took a deep dive to write about redemptive suffering, healing from childhood trauma ("To the Begotten, Not Made"). As I took refuge on a bed of twigs in the sand, the waves deposited matter into the sea and carried my cargo to rest ("Coquina Beach").

Healing is a long, hard thing. I come full circle back to the roots where "the tree lets go, knows a peace with living and dying" ("Back to the Roots"). I have come from a childhood with no memory before repeated rape—mentally before physically—to drifting aimlessly at sea in early adulthood and now to more than 35 years as an adult of therapeutic healing. I have scar tissue that I sometimes feel in the night. But the wound has healed, and the sickness will not go back into my head ("Sent into the Sea"). I know, no matter the loss, the wind-breath carries redemptive suffering ("Harboring Hope"). My debut full-length poetry collection, *Deep Dive*, celebrates the holy path of walking with courage, hope, and love.

—Karen Carter
June 23, 2024 – Winston-Salem, North Carolina

Talking Trees

I sit on my front porch.
This 71-degree heat calls for spring
to shed light on the shifting time.
I wonder what the trees are saying
to each other about war, peace—the war
in Ukraine. The trees have seen
it all—the fallen, the decay, the dead
thrown into the ground for seeds
to sprout, to spring once again.

Twelve tall trees stand
across the road
at the edge of the woods.
Trees, taller than the utility
lines in front of them,
bend every time
SW March wind, 21 mph, travels
so that the trees touch,
talk to each other.

Do the talking trees long
to inspire, stand still with resilience,
or will they erode from climate change?
Or do these trees feel like "I must do
something" when the wind bursts
return as they will in the next
few minutes.

Yes, now the wind shifts the talking
trees from standing still to breathing
into each other's space.
The trees in the center of the twelve,
the tallest, carry the swaying
of their brothers, sisters, like video shows
the real horrors of brothers, sisters, lives
lost on the battlefield, at home, in
make-shift shelters—no matter which side
they are on.
What do these talking trees say about nuclear
war power? About us?

The sun is out now.
The clouds shift, form a chain moving
slowly behind the trees, as once again,
the trees stand still.
Clouds, like puffy cotton balls, stretch
across the sky like a peace sign
to be disturbed or energized by wind gusts.
Do the talking trees know which one?
Is their talking perhaps diplomacy
for the world to follow?
Will it be empty speech
or a breath of hope?

In the Spirit of Emily Dickinson

I've never seen God,
but I've walked a trail,
a monarch butterfly
flapping in the wind.

I've never tasted glory,
but I've watched an Oklahoma sunset,
a big ball of fire
dying in the west.

I've never touched a star,
but I've sat on my roof,
drunk a bottle of merlot, eating goat cheese,
crunching saltine crackers.

I've never heard the whale's song,
but I've joined a Christmas chorus,
carolers in harmony door-to-door
as they carry the tune,
march in the snow.

I've never smelled a lover's breath
from long, slow kisses,
but I've lingered in the berry patch,
sucking wild strawberries,
tangy juice trickling down my throat.

Wear a White Rose

A white petal turns
paper seeds into leaflets,
eye-witness accounts
to stir human apathy into action,
decry Nazi genocide.

The White Rose Movement in 1943
is not silent, sweet, peaceful.
The flower paper tells the story,
plants the words Sophie Scholl
and her fellow medical students
and faculty advisor write
to record the stench of death.

A whiff of this graffiti
tells the truth.
The flower opens in the second leaflet,
strewn along the paths of resistance,
openly uncovers and denounces
atrocities of blond supremacy,
the mark of mass graves.

The flower-plant-paper calls
for disarmament of weapons
of mass destruction while the movement
lays to rest Sophie Scholl,
when she is betrayed, sent
to the Gestapo—German state
police—for execution February 22, 1943.

Today the white rose,
tucked in a lapel,
or pinned on a shirt,
reverence of the wounded spirit,
honors the dead
at funerals—everywhere,
all races and nationalities.
Wear a white rose.

When fear rises

I'm driving through a fog.
Home to public school, I
travel up and down hills,
the 45-mile-stretch
like an obstacle course
to test resolve.

I need this cloudy patch,
not as a puffy mattress,
but as an iron shield,
armor to keep
fear from taking over,
fear like punctured tires
draining all the energy
out of me before
I get going.

The fog moves
this way and that
like monstrous mutations,
mountain-sized mirrors.
I do not see the road
ahead. I hold on tight
to the wheel. The view
looks murky.

I slow down speed
rounding the curves,
check the impulse
to drive head
strong into the laced veil.
Breathe. Hold up the veil.

Let it fall like a marker,
the white line
in the center
of this country road.

If I didn't have this fog,
if I saw everything ahead,
instead of what is right
in front of me, the dip
in the road would cover
me up, like the bottom
dropping out from under.

I look forward to this drive.
The fear rises early
in the morning. Thick clouds
of tiny moisture patiently wait.
I'm on the road,
following a moving map,
no shortcuts, no turning back,
once I travel with this guide.

Deposited Deep

"I cried three hours,"
an old teacher says.
"I wept last night,"
a young teacher says,
"then again this morning
before school started."

The old teacher remembers,
says, "so much depends
on loss—years of academic
learning—now carried
to the sea, deposited deep
in the ocean floor.
Climate change,
"the struggle is real,"
experts say.

Real like mold
in 1970's school buildings
across the nation where air
circulates from a child's language,
muttering the "B" word
to a teacher fresh
out of college.

"I froze," she says.
Frozen, like an iceberg
waiting for the ship
to sink.

One Brief Moment

At home, after a doctor's visit,
I get out of my automobile,
see glittered threads streak
across the tops of autumn trees.
They move as quickly as the whiplash
I got earlier, only the impact left.

I had left the bank, my automobile
parked. I got in, strapped the seat belt.
Before turning the ignition key,
a truck pounded into the rear
of my vehicle. My seat belt on,
still I jerked.

Here at home, I do not look
for an autumn sunset. But turning
my head to the left, I see these
burnt-orange stripes light up the trees,
kiss the tops with their twinkling
star-struck reflection.

I need this angle of light to touch me.
But in one brief moment,
the sky's orange ball of fire drops
to the ground, gone from sight.
The flickers of flame disappear.

Would I await the energy's return
at tomorrow's dusk? Or is my loss,
I fear, the sharp pain in my neck
something more lasting than
nature's quick whiplash
from light to dark?

The evening stands still, waits
for day to die
while I hold on to memory,
take in the golden strands.
A different angle of beauty
now hides from view,
one brief moment
before the sun goes down.

Where a Turtle Leads

Get up. Curse the lie
murdering too long a reneged speech.
Dry hands cup simple ignorance,
piecemeal scant wisdom
from a rosy mouth glossing over
luminous death.

Tame the impulse to quit the night.
Let boredom fast
like rock salt melts ice.

Refuse to squash the brightness
of a turtle sitting idle,
its tiny head lowered for the distance.
It kicks its way forward,
busies itself to a crawl
up and down,
front and behind,
across the fields,
towards the sea,
where the heavens destroy dishonor.

Veins
—After *A Tree Within* by Octavio Paz

Come closer -
Can you hear it

I knew poetry would pour
out of my veins, what he calls
roots in his poem.
It took the pandemic for me
to set my own roots aflame.

Now the fire grows wild
like writing rips those veins
right out of my skin.

Maybe that's what Paz knew,
Day breaks
in the body's night.
There, within, inside my head,
the tree speaks.

My tree is like the tall oak,
never bends to fear
of life's weathered storms.
Let the blood flow.

Page Torn from Tea Leaves

I am from the diary,
refusing to open
private crevices,
my smudged-over lies.

I am from the green tea,
preserving life, exposing truth,
the kiwi pear and pineapple
ginger of gardened pleasures.

I am the writer, homeless
child, the longing of a constant
tree pruned from brittle branches,
no longer distanced from the wind
breathing mass into the rib.

Between Being and Doing

Curly-haired child sits in diapers
on linoleum kitchen floor,
opens enamel stove drawer and peeks,
collects aluminum, steel pots and pans,
hugs them against her bare chest.

Adult female plays with wooden cubes,
makes Freudian slips on soft pillows.
In her therapist's office of carpeted chairs,
she clutches reality with her checkbook,
enters a space destined for healing.

Writing disciplines her;
sessions throw darts at dulled senses,
focus the mind to hit the bulls-eye,
create respect for the pen.

In the stuff of child's play with pots and pans,
an adult's coming to terms with stages and ages,
space between dreams and language,
the pen waits to grasp the common word.

November Cloak

Auntie Jane's blanket,
attic-stored for air cloves,
with her knitted cable yarn
she hums a morning tune.

Notes of royal blue, cream,
black, sunshine yellow,
strike a melody,
like a peacock trimmed in fringe.
Her knotted threads weave a story.

Careful folds
hang over a wooden chair,
a life layered
in gentle pursuit.

Her tiny cross stitches,
her nimble fingers,
her ponderings of the mind,
her eyes set,
frame each fabric.

I swing my shoulders
into her charm,
wrap her memories,
hug them against my bare chest—
cuddle—coat—coo—like a newborn
dove breathes life, a lamb rests,
enveloped in nature's bed.

I cup my sleeves of hot chocolate,
marsh-mellowed hands
inside her cloak
to brush and caress her layered patterns,
like fresh fallen leaves color autumn hair.
Like soft cotton-candy wool,
her art sketches a worn path.

Auntie Jane, with each square,
names a quilt of kindred spirits.
A little more than a century and a half ago,
women hearth-sitting,
stitch a way to freedom.

Turn Signals

Earth's gentle turning looks
like a dozen raspberry-coated
yellow buds, roses opening
up in their puberty.

A phone-charger cord connects
to its roots after a ding.
The message pops up,
15% battery.

Stacks of graded papers pile
high like a mass of bees
return to the hive, play different roles,
ready to work another day, ready to sting
if someone steps on them.

A slice of butter-colored moon,
a waxing crescent, looms over
my auto while I travel before daylight.
My headlights and a signal on my auto
that says BRAKE keep me from hitting
a motorcycle rider sputtering 30 mph
right in front of me.

Night falls to day
like a cockroach kicks up
on its back on the kitchen tile,
alive but poisoned by bug spray.

A mouth gushed with sweet watermelon
curbs morning thirst.

A floater in my eye crawls
back and forth like a black widow spider
decides where to land.

In the early morning daylight,
men wearing orange, safety vests
weed out tall, fresh cut grass
along the side of the road.
Their stand-up weed cutters swing
left and right like genies out of the bottle
blow stardust from their hands across the sky
to make a wish come true.

I travel. After a wax job, the shiny black tires
on my automobile spin like a wash
in the machine. Newly paved
roads cover up potholes.

As the day turns to night,
another slice of butter-colored moon,
a waxing crescent, spotlights
a Mama bear and cubs. They raise
their heads, sink their bodies
into the stalks of the mowed corn
patch in the field next to my house.

Thanksgiving

Time tossed, the day idle,

Harvest moon shines pregnant.

Apple crisp air

Nestles, sleeps, snores.

Kerosene lamp flickers, like a shadow

Sways in the moonlight. Memory induces

Giant dreams; sighs exhale.

I watch the glow,

Velvet soft, like a puff of wind echoes.

I wonder how silent, how still

Night falls.

Grandfather clock ticks like an owl's wings

       muffle sound, calm nocturnal flight.

Nameless Tumbleweeds

Records retreat
like tumbleweeds in the desert
blow deeds into nameless blocks.

A door thinks the heart walks out
to leave its misty valleys.
But the key turns
to face its nameless fears.

Restless minds forsake names,
like frost dirt hardens
to white, icy cold mass.

Decay skims the empty book pages,
where chalk and pen have left the house.
The classroom board and library sit
quiet, still.

Earth listens,
holds it breath, waits,
then exhales, speaks,
releases its tears.

Sacred Land

Water splashes over jaded cliffs,
creviced between tall trees;
twigs carry storied rafts
down a muddy stream.

Sunlight fades
over worn mountains,
aged by silenced tongues.

Snow and clouds
stretch across sky's view,
shade time and river's flow.

High above the holy ground,
wrinkled faces, drawn lips brood,
protect the indigenous vision.

Rays of headdresses
spotlight legends on watered rock;
feathers connect
high and low tangled places.

No one dares to walk
where light shines
on buried spaces.

Winter Breath

Deer in the headlights stop,
dazed by the moon's beams.
Mottled hair shoots
straight up, legs wonder
where to go next.

An icicle droops
from the roof-top house,
not knowing where the freeze
will take it.
But the icicle is content
to showcase art—if not
for a moment—before it melts
in the noonday sun.

At night, shadows pass
like silhouettes press
against the wall, hide
from human view, wait
for vanity to be swept
away as soot for the fireplace.

The fireplace, stocked
with cargos of logged grief,
calls the reader to take a break
from inflamed ego,
hibernate so that silence may speak.

The woodpiles stack
themselves higher at each end,
serve as bookends,
containers for chaos and creation
from the pages read.

The cold and the night forecast
a time to surrender:
fast plans of the deer,
eternal space of the icicle,
heavy logs of the inflamed fire,
and vanity of the human.

Slate Blue

Sky fades behind clouds
tumbling like hills, hiding
the promise of sun.

Slates of winter ice glaze the field,
cast shadows on barren trees,
expose brittle branches,
ready to snap,
if wind-power lifts the air.

From my front view,
this wintry mix
the blue of the sofa
in my living room, decades old,
knocked about, its arms worn
slick from tears of lonesome dreams.

Outdoors,
a tree stands alone.
Its two branches—shaped like a V—rise
high from the trunk.
The tree waits
for something to bloom
or for the V to come together somehow,
the two joined in one,
in a holy union,
like a wooden pencil I hold
in my hand in front of me.

I move the pencil
back and forth in a straight line
to see if it is one or two.

When it becomes one,
my vision sharpens,
corrects astigmatism,
the experts say.

I miss the tree
without its leafy branches of fertility,
though I am grateful
for the tree itself,
as barren as it must be in winter.

I know I must wait until spring decides
to enter my muted palette.
Winter settles, not yet ready
for sky blue to let the clouds break
through my rest.
Perhaps it suits me just fine,
solace with aloneness,
time out,
not yet ready for the excitement
of spring's social butterfly days
and its bumble bee chat or even summer's
lightning bug night.

Awakened
(Red Tulips)

Red tulips, isolated in a plant bed
on a city street corner, rise
high like a lone petal grows
inches in a crack in the sidewalk.

One flower like a meadow of dreams
wakes me up, dares
me to forget my auto-pilot pace,
exchange my plans of a daily, busy routine
for a stop on a brisk morning walk.

A little frost last night,
maybe that's why the flower stands
tall but not straight up. Perhaps
it reaches out to me
like a person faces forward
when it's time for me to pay attention.

The red blooms rush
blood in my veins,
give me water to drink
so someone can draw
my blood later on in a lab today.

For now, I sit.
Red tulips, you awaken me.
I don't want to be like the tourist
that snaps a pic of beauty
with a camera phone
and quickly moves on.

I want to feel your petals shaking
in the breeze, hold my head high,
inhale the fertile, plant-based soil
that attracts little bugs crawling
to get a taste of the good life.

Behind me I hear the sound of trash
pickup rise above the birdsong.
Still, you collect my thoughts,
channel them into "here".

Oh, how many times I have longed
to be present with someone.
But I turn my head away from you
to see an ornate grey concrete slab
shaped like a bathtub with soil
but no plants in it.
Is the soil doing something?
Why are there no plants?
The container makes me feel sterile.

I turn back to you, red tulips,
as if you are tilting your head,
extending your petals for a handshake,
or pressing your red lips
on me for a kiss.

But it is enough for me to sit
with you without the need to touch.

Together—we breathe in,
breathe out—the crisp morning air.

Later, I will not need a coffee
because in this moment in time
I drink the reddest wine of the chalice.

Kick the Can

I heard mortality was coming
like a hot, slow-cooker day
gives way to a weeping rainfall,
fills a water jug in the shade,
the bucket in a vanishing forest.

Memories drift like water,
a distant admiration for little streams
to run down stony ground.

A black bear disturbs
death's jealous room
of ubiquity.
I hear the sound, kick the can,
the trash bin at the edge
of the gravel driveway turned over.
I go to my front door, see the big
fellow with a white plastic bag
in its mouth. The bear tears it open,
dips into some left-over
cheese dip.

An automobile runs down
the country road. The bear races along
the side of the car, holds on
to the food bag, rushes into the woods.

When my brother Bill and I were kids,
we played outdoors until dark,
entertaining ourselves with Kick the Can,
hide and seek, lost and found games.

Bill got into everything, like the time
he poked a stick in a bush in the front
yard. The bees buzzed out and stung
him. I watched him run.

I hear my brother died in his recliner,
his dog by his side.
Tonight, when mortality kicks the can,
it appears like a familiar ghost,
packs nothing,
departs with human finitude.

The Unfettered Life

Each day by the lake,
geese fly along the walker's trail.
Today a goose flies through the trees
across the city pond.

I'm on my fifteen-minute work break
away from the sales, the cold calls,
125 I'm required to make a day.

But here in the shade, I stand on the bank,
watch a goose glide towards me,
a creature unfettered I long to be.

While I think, I need this job,
the goose turns its head, slants its body,
curves to the right, extends its long crawl,
clips, catches its shadow, coasting.

A holding pattern? Me? It?
Does the goose prep for the perfect landing?
Can I buy time to get out of this dead-end job?

The goose ascends, spreads its wings,
white over black feathers.
I confess, I have a lot to learn before I succeed,
like maybe even getting to work on time.

I watch the goose descend.
I flinch when it lands not inches from me.
Did it brush my shoulder?

The goose waits, its feet flat on the ground.
I reach into my jean pocket, take out a pouch of kernels.
I feed it corn,
its morning treat.

Forgiven

Homemade peach ice cream churns,
spoons its sweet milk.
Ice cubes rattle,
release the cool breath of spring,

A pool of clear aqua,
coupled with my breast strokes,
drains my mind's cobwebs.

Kites strung on a bright orange sunset
erase mistakes across the sky.

Self-love is a hard thing.
Always looking back
turns Lot's wife into a pillar of salt.
Fear sometimes makes me dive
off the board with a belly splash.
But more often I dive deep,
enough to push me up for air-filtered breath.

Lightning bugs flash night's constellation.
The moon accepts my frightened stares,
long enough for suffering to tolerate pain
in order to understand it.
Its time-released energy drives
tomorrow's swimming laps.

Ladybug Blues

Ladybug in the Bathroom

When doing what you love
feels like a chore,
when a ladybug
crawls up the drain pipe,
plops on the bathroom
sink. She finds the faucet,
tucks in her legs,
hunkers down for a good old nap.

It's spring,
or the not-yet, maybe in-between
time after hibernating
in winter. She has to figure out
where to lay all those eggs.

She may just stay in the house,
content—unless some sudden
movement upsets her.
And she quickly releases
a yellow fluid, which stains
the bathroom wall.
She hasn't traveled far from
the faucet to the wall,
but wandering
can take its toll.

Where are her friends?
No insects swarm in the house.
She's solitary, all alone
in adventure, her flight
up the drain pipe.
Was it worth it?

Ladybug in the Kitchen

Somehow this ladybug has made it
from the bathroom to the kitchen
for a little sleep, warmth,
and a safe place.

No small beetles around,
no partner, the ladybug retreats
into the interior.
Just sits—inactive
no need to run.

Perhaps the ladybug sings the blues
for mating woes.
Knows she does not mate for life.
Males come and go, her having
plenty of choices and chances
to produce all those eggs.

But why has she taken a break,
sought refuge here?

The cold makes the ladybug chill,
even face the death of winter.

With keen eyesight, she leans in
to the light.

A little light might draw
her out of herself—especially if
sporting red on her skin,
a sign of friendship and partnership.

But danger awaits her cozy shelter,
threatens her refugee status at the table.
Citrus, cloves, mums,
bay leaves, peppermint,
lavender—these scents drive
her away.

She is harmless, carries no deadly
disease. But the kitchen counter
or encounter can destroy her camp.
A spray of white vinegar can kill,
right on the spot.

Ladybug in the Garden

There is a way for the ladybug
to do what she loves even when
it feels like a chore.
She can work out of this funk
(live) no longer food insecure
when she returns to the outdoors.

Perhaps a journey from the kitchen
window out onto the garden
gives chance
to practice vocation.

A feast awaits her in the garden.
She joins her comrades,
becomes the Best Bud Bug
of the gardener—when she eats
aphids—the gardener's mortal enemy.
She can make a meal out of aphids,
mites, and scale, by herself,
eat 50 or more aphids each day,
keeping that pest control intact
with fine dining on white flies
and mealybugs too.

A trip up the drain pipe, up onto the
bathroom sink and faucet, she has
made it to the kitchen for a short respite.
Now out back under the window, she finds
the outdoors. In the garden,
she's in paradise.

Citrus Delight

Green and red grapes, peaches, pears,
sweet cherries overflow
my turned maple bowl
like peacock's wings outspread.

Fingers sprinkle shredded coconut;
hug round orange,
peel its pith.
Juice dresses apple skin.

Ruby grapefruit strings
wedges between my teeth.
A slice of mandarin
orange coats my palate.

Citrus tickles my throat.
My succulent dreams come true.

Front Porch Sitting

Day 27 of Quarantine
A tiny, brown lizard crawls up
my front porch steps,
jerking its head turning back and forth.
Then, content to play dead,
the reptile spreads out its extremities,
plants them firmly on the brick.
I drink my morning ginger peach hot tea.

Some time passes. I know not how long.
Without notice, the little lizard slides
down the porch,
like the green grass of spring
calls its curiosity to dance.

To the right of my open porch,
a spider web hangs from the azalea bush.
Notched by four corners,
rectangular threaded holes sway in web delight,
like a dream catcher shoulders
the previous night's fright,
awakens a new morning dew.

I hear the sounds, "Woo WOO Woo,"
the second woo pitched a little higher.
Is this the Great Horned Owl in the woods?
The wise one that activated the motion
light on my front porch Halloween night?
The eyes that penetrated me,
then flew to sit on my backyard clothes line?
The owl now revisiting me?

My front porch sitting redeems a lost art,
though some may say my quiet,
gentle pursuit, greeting
the social pleasures of a new day,
simply masks piddling.

I feel a wind stirring
silence between my toes.
Perhaps lizard, spider, and Great Horned Owl
check in on me—my life turned inward—while I
check them out.

Solitude

The wind whispers a welcome wandering,
here in COVID-19, here in the quarantine.

A bumble bee dances around the clematis,
while a black-yellow butterfly tastes
the first fruits of spring.

The woodpecker drums;
its pecking hammers nails into hollow hearts.
The putt-putt sound in woodland trees,
the bass of the drum,
carry the echo of a tadpole
launching onto a paper plate,
trash someone threw in the water ditch,
which usually holds drainage
anticipating the next hurricane.
But today the plate serves up
a lily pad for the frog
while the hurricanes
rest until summer.
Songbird awaits robins in the trees
to pitch a tune, make a melody.
Red cardinals dip their beaks
into the rich, moist sod to wipe their bills,
like using a napkin to clean themselves
or spraying mist with a cologne spritzer.

The eyes of a dragonfly detect my wonder;
its vision captures every inscrutable detail of my life.
The dragonfly senses movement
in the stillness of the moment,
while its see-through, thread-like airplane wings
and dainty legs rest on my tea cup.

The Great Monarch Migration

Today travel restrictions
keep tourists away from the Great Monarch Migration.
But two men linked to the butterfly reserve,
outspoken to illegal logging in the forest,
have died, their bodies found here in Angangueo,
Mexico,
their deaths in February 2020 concealed in mystery.

My friend, world traveler of historic sites,
shows me pictures of Angangueo, Mexico,
a mining town northwest of Mexico City,
where tourists in buses once photographed
the procession of the monarchs.

Why do the monarchs perch?
Billions of butterflies
kneel and bend to nectar,
watch and wait on every branch and bush.

I look at the photos a second time.
I wonder why feather-like creatures
once cross the busy cities and today's deserts,
fly on bright, sunny days.
Escape the cold, experts say, but why
do the monarchs feast and die?
Habitat loss, climate change?

She whispers,
"No one knows."
But it is forbidden to trap butterflies there.
So many flutter, flail, and flap.

I study the pictures a third time and say,
"Their shadows hide the mountain's greenery."
Pigmented scales diffract
ultraviolet light,
undetectable to the human eye.

The butterflies feast,
cluster on nature's branches.
Tree limbs crack,
collapse under the insects' beating breaths.

She shows me more photos.
Back then, nearby, outside a church,
a woman kneels and weeps after confession.
Lilies stand at the base of the crucifix.

The Mexican flag drapes our communion table.
The red silk reminds me of the Hill of Golgotha,
the blood spilled after one last drink and Jesus nailed,
the green, a heritage to sanctuary.

My friend and I sip Mexican tea.
She shows me the rocky road,
her hour's climb uphill
long ago to see the butterflies.

Dragonfly

I sit on my open front porch
15 months after teaching public school
all things remote and hybrid.
I am going back to school in person,
but I remember
how unsettled I was.

Mid-July 2020—a decision to make—do I go
back to public school?
I said to the dragonfly,
I am 68, asthma-fixed.
Teaching—my vocation, my higher calling—
I am pretty good at it.

Outdoors, here on my front porch,
ginger peach tea settles my stomach.
The dragonfly sits on my tea cup and I in my chair.
Grief looks like a strain,
my neck turned sideways.
I just want to get closer to the dragonfly.

The dragonfly's head fascinates me.
How does a big head attach to a tiny neck?
The dragonfly's head, designed for mobility,
circles around a center point,
like a robot in a chemist's lab during quarantine.
The chemist, sheltered in place,
searches for a vaccine,
runs experiments on a laptop,
while the head of a dragonfly
does the grunt work.

Light speed, eyeballing, it moves.
The dragonfly lines up
the glass vials, sorts them;
no doubt an essential worker, a vital organ,
this head of a dragonfly,
this tough, rounded capsule.

With its four sets of threaded airplane wings,
dainty and delicate,
like its thorax, the dragonfly can lift itself up.
Will I?
Will the dragonfly take off
faster than rocket speed?
But I digress.
For now, the dragonfly rests on my tea cup.

The dragonfly's robot-head rotates,
like when I fill out a teacher survey
on how to go back to public school safely,
or enroll in a teacher online course—how to teach—all
things remote learning.
"I am not a robot," I click, and the dragonfly's head
rolls around, like it is doing now on my tea cup.
It rolls around and around until I get it right,
get the answer, the go-ahead.
I'm in. I'm legit, no fake teacher here, no identity theft.

Oh, dear dragonfly, tell me more.
Observe me.
Unless I get this right, choose not to retire,
go back to public school, I am not the chemist,
sitting on my front porch.

I am the dragonfly.
But unlike you, this moment,
I am not settled, have not decided.
My big head does not attach to my little neck.
It hurts, like a toe dangling from a foot.

My dear dragonfly,
what do your eyes see?

Hope seals the virus

Little red coats,
their black masks pushed up,
the cardinals absorb droplets.
Their little beaks
get tampered, trampled
in an avalanche of snow.
Yet they dip to find a crumb.

Not much food to eat or want
from a tasteless fever, no smell,
as a COVID nurse turns
a patient in the bed every two hours.

Still the little birds wait to sing.

Talk to me through a glass cube
because unmasked you cannot enter
my classroom. I dip my mouth,
chin up, speak a gargled,
masked sound of teacher talk.
I give my students my best.
After reading Robert Frost's
"After Apple Picking," they tell
me, they are tired of apples,
tired of school.

Still
Hope holds on, hunkers down,
parades through the barren belief.
The cardinals call
out the fragile footing of the present.

Saturday morning, I
stand in front of my kitchen window,
wash dishes I should have washed
the night before.
A beautiful Northern Cardinal
canvases the ground,
searching for food.

I think,
what if this creature's sweet song
gets silenced, perhaps injured
from hitting a car window
or a pane on the house?

ARDS Acute Respiratory Distress Syndrome

Interviewed in a national, daily newspaper,
a COVID nurse explains proning.
To breathe: Place the patient belly down
on the bed.
Ten months after his first case,
he says he does not feel like the best nurse.
But focus on the life-sustaining stuff, he says.

The injured bird with its little red coat on
cannot stand on its own,
land on its feet.
Grab a shoe box with holes in it
so the bird can breathe.
With gloves on, place the cardinal
on a heating pad in the shoe box.
Add shredded tissue paper for comfort.

Let it rest.
Call the wildlife rehabilitation facility.

The COVID nurse finds
a ventilator for his patient.
Rest.
Wait.
Pray.

Today this COVID nurse
takes his first dose
of the vaccine.

We wait
for the virus to find
its own box.
Seal it tightly, says Hope.

Desolate

Framed diploma and teacher's license,
taped on the institutional wall,
these credentials face the stars.
The star-struck welcome board posts a message:
Practice safety.
But will these stars fade, fall into the waste basket?

No.
Hand sanitize the room,
cherish the stars like "Hope
is the thing with feathers," says Emily Dickinson.
But the Dickinson banner is losing some of its red-
colored shapes,
while it looks up to the battery-operated clock.
Pandemic time ticks
like paper-made dreams sleep, stashed away, on file.

No.
Pull these dreams out of the file cabinet.
Spread them like the real peacock feathers,
retrieved from the farm.
They fly high on the dry erase black board.
The eyes of the feathers point to the sky,
chalk and eraser ready for pick up.

No.
Room keys dangle on noodled paper chains.
Tasks crumple up into paper sacks of worn masks
quarantined,
teacher's desk pristine,
no papers in sight, all things remote,

like a train of passengers stuck in empty box cars,
or sailors stuck at sea for seasons,
waiting.

No.
That's not for you.
Flag the muse.
Contact trace your purse and chair.
Lie back to embrace silence
like smelling wood,
nose pinned to the pages of a new book
when you first open it.
Head outdoors.
Breathe deeply
beneath your kn95.
Pick up a yellow legal pad,
number 2 pencil.
On your mark, get set.
Write.

First Bells

At school, I check my temperature,
waiting for the mechanic voice to let me
enter the school house, the same monotone
each day to gnaw at me with authority.
"Temperature normal," it registers me,
usually 97.34.

School bells clang like my ocean
blue stainless steel coffee thermos
dings against my classroom keys
dangling around my neck
on a school-coded lanyard.

Some days these keys hang like a sloth,
my feet shuffling,
my head turning upside down from noise.

Most days the bells clamor
like an alarm clock tossing
me out of bed so fast
I have to tuck the sheets back
under the mattress, before
I gulp down my first cup of dark roast coffee.

The first cup of coffee is like a first kiss,
simple, short, not penetrating,
just sweet enough to long for more,
but not too long to linger with an aftertaste
of too sweet, like a honey bun,
or too stale, like expired dark chocolate.
I brush my teeth.

I clock in at the main office's
thump, thump, thump 30-year-old
keyboard. The last four numbers of my social
security I pound on it, before I head outdoors
across the lawn to the next building.

Today my principal jokes from a distance
with a teacher whose car bells
will not stop ringing,
like a tardy bell keeps screeching.
She shouts back,
"I can't turn it off. My keys are locked
inside my car."

Somehow the car alarm halts all traffic.
I enter the building with the school bells ringing,
this time, like waves disturbed
from silence rush ashore,
or like a hammer hits
the first nails of a new frame,
reverberating at 7:55 a.m.
when the new day begins,
first bells.

Time Capsule

Rose petals fall to the ground,
not caring what phase it is of the pandemic.
Hands prune the vine, clear a space
for the roots to stay,
release vaccines.

Raw talent carries thorns,
packed in the artist's pocket trousers,
while an oil painting hangs
on a museum wall, uncovers
the next chokehold.

Writer's thoughts, alone and isolated,
carry volumes,
like vignettes collect patches of dust,
waiting for its time capsule's release.
Businesses and schools re-open.
Small buds for blooms
take their chances.

Released, her poems blossom,
The painter frames his work,
labored in unnatural time.
But for now, the writer,
self-isolated, connects
words on paper, plots
scenes to collaborate stories, waits
for resolution, holdings
from vast storage of the mind.

The library opens up, a garden,
laden with books,
records the mourning,
spreads the seed from the fallen,
mass graves,
so the roses will breathe.

Back to the Roots

My heart aches
to be like a tree swinging
its willowy branches in faint, misty air.
After a storm, my tree travels
like a rainbow stretches
its pastel green, yellow, peach
hues across the sky.

My tree, its foliage free to change,
needs less sunlight,
embraces the sunset years,
stops the food-making work production
of the leaves' younger years,
but still finds the courage
to fortify a solid trunk.

The tree lets go,
knows a peace
with living and dying.
It releases its red-orange-yellow leaves
that once showcased beauty.

My tree sings like a singer
in an orchestrated symphony,
the melody of the swan song
as the leaves drop deep
into fertile soil, make a path,
new seeds to grow.

I no longer need
a mustard seed to grow.
My interior tells me,
the time has come to shed the exterior,
like the full-blown tree knows
it must give up its centerpiece
cornucopia, its fruits and flowers,
so that the tree returns to its roots.

The Bridge

A stream cries
for wooden planks caressed with rope
to greet an adventurous traveler,
commune with the tree tops,
reach hands to the sky,
walk deliberate steps in moccasin soles,
tip a safari hat to nature's blossoms.

Fresh air absorbs morning dew.
Birds chirp to announce the dawn
the closing of the gap
between unknown territories
beckoning the wanderer.

Rise Up Geranium Word-Gems
(Pelargoniums)

My geraniums cry out
for water to quench their thirst
like my words wait
in the sanctuary of my mind,
ready to sprout on the blank page,
once a pinch of the pencil
or a snip of the keyboard
shapes the word-gems
into stem stanzas.

"Water them like they're dying,"
says the high school agriculture teacher,
who gave me these sturdy green
Pelargoniums, root-bound
like my words tightly packed
into economized poems.
I make every word count
so the poem-plant grows
like well-nourished leaves
lap up dignity.

The hand that pours the water
must be careful not to overdo,
overwork the poem with
interpretation. Trust the words
to carry the narrative
because word-gems, like geraniums,
die in soggy soil.

Mind the moisture
with drainage holes in the container
so the potting mix does not rot.
Only water the top inch of the soil.

Word-gems need editing,
extra words cut, the poem contained,
the bare minimum written
to grow from
the stem stanza
into bushy leaves, flowers.

Too much wetness for too long
in the pot without the drainage
makes the leaves fall over,
the plant no longer able to rise up.

Poems need the muse.
Geraniums need full sun,
six to eight hours a day,
but not too much summer heat.

I move the container for afternoon shade
so the leaves do not drop, so my words
stay crisp with revision and rest.

Today I sit on my front porch,
see for the first time in four weeks
peach blossoms.
I hope care colors my work.

Painting Words

Cumulus clouds stretch
across the sky
like detached cauliflower
line up for a fair
weather forecast.

I lie flat on a beach towel,
another towel I bundle
for a head prop.
I arch my feet,
plant them
in the stirrups of the sand.

Looking up, I see in the sky
a scene that looks like
fish scales, a jaw-breaking
mouth slating the clouds
as they disperse
like a sheet of ice
punctures an inflated balloon.

Who knows where the imagination
takes the creative
glued to the sand
while a small plane with a huge sign
flies overhead, advertises
airplane rides with numbers (I can read
even without my glasses on).

Planting words
for the creative
is like lying still
to inhale and exhale
silence
while words emitted
paint a picture
into poems.

A Forecast of Severe Storms Today

Shorebirds glide in formation,
twice circling the water crests,
not ready to land in search of food.
They shape the sky like their canopy-laced
feathers cover the water bed
inches above the sea.
These little birds repeat their routine,
flap their wings,
while waves thunder
in rolls, crash along the shore.

Youth sport a volleyball game.
Feet firmly planted in the sand,
one player jumps to make a kill,
slips into a fall.

The volleyball spins
now that the wind
has picked up speed.
Adults inclined on sand dunes
watch the play.

Why does the ocean pay
no attention to the audience?
The waves roll, crest, break,
moment by moment,
infinite in movement.
The wind bursts with thunderous
roar whether anyone
is there or not to heed the call.

The flyover of the birds,
the symphony of the waves,
the orchestrated breath of the wind
keep on into infinity while
creatures, even in danger
of human extinction,
like the Ukrainian musicians,
tour across Europe in concert.

Lullaby

I rest on a sand dune, hear the lullaby.
Rolling waves sing their hush
like a clock's two-movement tick tock
times each hour into eternity.

The wavelength sways back and forth,
quiets my thinking, quivering hands
as I gather a cup of sand,
sift it through my fingers
like the ocean waves to the shoreline
bury weightless footprints littered
along the trail.

Orange hues across the ocean sky
release the brief day into evening light
to signal night is nigh.

I listen, I see the moon
and the moon sees me.
The moon sees who I want to see.

The night settles
scores of lost dreams,
leaks memories for the moon
to find a place, a home for them
like neatly, folded clean shirts
fall out of a beach bag,
ask the traveler to pack and unpack
again, not forgetting torn sandals,
for light travel in the morning.

For now, it is enough to go asleep
to the lullaby of the clock's tick tock,
the hourglass sand timer,
the moonlit dreams,
and the waves in chorus.

Ocean Surfing

A seagull shimmers through the air,
its feather-fan like a fanny of shredded
tissue paper, ready to wrap itself up
lightly through crosscurrents.

The long-winged bird goes for the distance,
glides over the ocean, searches
for food, while rip currents wash back
dead things to lie on the shore.

The gull dips its beak, stout
like a clump of sand, wet
by the give and take of the ocean waves.
Gulp.
The bird tastes the little fragments,
chunks from its longing,
like a little boy runs
around his sand castle, inspects it
for afternoon flight.

The gulls look
weightless, hovering
over the ocean. The little boy's castle,
full of wet sand, stands high
like a fortress.

He steps up on the mound,
plants one leg in front of the other,
extends his arms like the gulls
fly in formation over the water,
their helicopter movement
a maneuver for balance.

The boy yells, YES!
He glides down the sand castle
on his surfboard, reaching a smooth landing.

Excited, like when the gulls start crying,
screaming, the boy rushes with his surfboard
under his arm, ready to do it again.
This time he gets a clump of sand in his mouth
when he makes the fall.

A running dive—the gulls, the boy—they
both turn somersaults in the air.

The rip currents, strong today,
invite the ocean waves to sound
their own boisterous drumbeat.
The gulls slide over the ocean
in silence.

The boy hears the adults say,
time to go home.

The waves weigh in, saying:
Dive like there's no tomorrow,
but never forget the ocean
turns moments into eternity.

Return tomorrow to the shore.

Body Splash

When you are 65+ years old,
every year at the annual physical,
the nurse asks,
"Have you had a fall in the past year?"

Here at the ocean,
the waves, drenched in seaweed
foam, splash a body to the shore,
dead or alive.

Aging is like falling,
waves cresting, bulging, breaking,
energy with a deep trough,
the reason for the nurse's question.

Day-by-day loss of memory
of ordinary things, falling
is like forgetting a place or a name,
even when one is mentally sharp.

I slip and slide on the wet sand,
extend my arms like wings,
or maybe like walking on a tightrope.
If I slip, I may go under
the rug of the ocean floor.

I feel the rush, when a bucket of water
splashes on me, makes me take a knee.
I did not see it coming.

To the Begotten, not Made

Ocean waves do not speak a language
of a tumbling ghost
or a beaten-down ache.

There was a time
I swam
a sea of meaningless
put-your-head-down, not
coming-up-for-air strokes.
I was hoping for hope in endless
hours of depressed wave-length toss,
searching for love
in broken, fragmented seashells.
Life scared me.
I was like a naked body
washed ashore,
pulled down by the rip currents,
a body floating the dead man's float,
a feat I learned to do well as a child,
fingers locked together
like a prison of seaweed
twisted and torn
with a rancor odor
not even bathing could cleanse.

My fragmented self
of the traumatized person
knew no beginning and end
veiled in eternity.

I would not go to the ocean
until I aged, until my 60's,

because fear writ large
smothered me like a speck of sand
doused over and over again
by waves breaking to shore.

Healing from trauma
is a long, hard thing.
The holy path never leaves me,
even when I mentally vacate.
The waves never stop
even when I want them to,
to once and for all engulf my pain,
release me,
let me transfer my cargo
to the waves' rumble.
But the waves never let up.

Now as I approach 70,
I believe the waves will not tell me
what to see,
will not sound off
what I should hear
because to take the highway into
the unseen, the unheard of,
I must sit with sorrow,
my feet covered up
by wet sand from the morning rain.

I listen to the ocean sounds.
I look into the ocean
with no sight of land in front of me.

I release my sobs without shame
to the Begotten, not Made
while the waves roll on
into eternity.

Sent into the Sea

Jesus sent the pigs into the sea
after cleansing
the Gerasene demoniac (Mark 5:13).

As a child, I would say to the pigs,
"Move out of my way,"
when I poured a bucket
of slop in the trough,

watched them gobble,
kick each other,
grunt and squeal
when they didn't get their way.

Last week stirred
memories of scapegoating violence.

As a child, my mind was raped
before my body.
I knew no theories, no way to drive
demonic suffering into the sea.

Decades later, I take deep breaths
here at the ocean.
My mind, restored to sanity,
still has times when nagging
negative fantasies,
a fear of scapegoating,
occupy space in my head,
the "what if" future.

I choose to walk
along the shore, dig
my feet into the sand.
I choose to drive those pigs
right into the sea.

I watch a gull dive
straight into the ocean.
Two black birds walk
up and down the shore,
dip their beaks into the sand,
come up with food.

The waves deposit matter
into the sea.

Coquina Beach

Broken seashells of coquina dot
the Cape Hatteras National Seashore.
A breeze gently sweeps holy whispers
along Coquina Beach,
like a fine-tooth comb grasps hair.
It scoops up moist earth.
Murals of wind stamp their footprints
in the charcoal-gray limestone sand.

The wind gusts,
shaking little tangle-free twigs in their roots.
They drift onto a shaded patch,
settle on a sun-streaked canvas of sand.

Then
blue-bowl swirls of sky
burst upon the water.
The waves tumble and crest—like an audience claps
its hands in delight—to applaud the artistry.
The painter waits to paint.

Little birds dip their beaks into the water
but rush away when the waves engulf them.
Then the tiny creatures go right back to eat something
the ocean has washed ashore.

Will the beachcomber spot the colorful coquina,
the moon snails, scallops, starfish, or perhaps a sand dollar
along the ocean wash?

I walk along the shore.
My feet take in the cool breath
of the limestone sand between my toes.
I find the spot where the twigs lay bare
the mattress of colorful coquina.
I notice the sand dunes.
They mark four corners
like a canopy bed held together by four posts.
I incline on one of the sand dunes,
hear the wind-blown whispers, "rest".

I watch some waves crash as they practice their craft.
A few waves pitch themselves higher than the rest.
A few more dot over the water
like a strand of pearls, strung in a half moon
until the rushing wind breaks them ashore.
The waves glide to shore, then stop,
like airplanes unloading their cargo.
I inhale and exhale like the planes coming to a halt.

Suddenly,
a new mural arrives from the public beach entrance.
Between two patches of sand dunes,
I see a pack of horses with riders descend onto the scene.
The horses line up, bow their heads to the roaring waves.
One by one each horse swishes its tail, clicks its heels,
stirs up sand, turns right, and gallops along the shore.
The rider rides the horse.

But look!
In this zone, completely free of commercial development,
an endless stretch of sand to the natural dune line,

a swimmer comes up to me in my canopy space
and holds up something.

"Look at this," he says. "A plastic flower, the ocean brought it."

He carries the green-stem, white lily—like it is an explosive—
off the beach.
He returns empty handed.

While the sun sets,
I wonder about a plastic flower bobbling
in the ocean.
Just how far has it traveled?
From where? When?
What is its footprint?

With its wind breath, the ocean breathes.
It gives life; it takes life.
It paints the natural coquina on the shore,
transfers and transforms it
into a bedrock of balm.
I close my eyes. I feel the murals of wind wrap around me
like a blanket that soothes and comforts the grieving soul.
I listen for the sounds of the waves gliding my own cargo to rest.

Harboring Hope

I'm turning off the TV, news of migrants
barred at the border, because
it's June—like a school-out party—time for ice cream.
Still, my thoughts turn
to asylum seekers,
longing—to taste what I am holding.
My homemade, banana ice cream churns
in a stone-cold, stainless steel jug.
The vitamin D whole milk creamed,
my frosty crystallizes
on a caramel waffle cone
as I take my first lick.

It's hot; it's June.
A few strawberries on top of my cone slide down.
My mind wanders
to a little girl treading
the murky waters of the Rio Grande.
I've never seen this natural river,
known for its bird migration path
and source of fresh water.
But I am hearing,
a little girl, with her arms flailing,
swims and walks in raw sewage,
nature's river now polluted.
Will she reach the Mexico-U.S. border?
I quickly lick more of my ice cream,
savoring the berry.

June—like a boiling pot—rises.
Summer swelters its heat on the weary trodden.

The little girl hears the migrants say,
about the "Rio Bravo del Norte,"
"mighty," but "furious" or "agitated,"
because the river's fast-flowing currents twist and turn,
unsettling to the refugee.
Still
the traveling companions head to the sandy shore.
The mouth of the Rio Grande opens up,
swallowing the wall-to-wall traffickers,
split apart by papers
or the lack of them.

But there's a festival at the town square.
I hear the carousel music, the organ announcing the circus.
Carnival rides show up
with politicians on merry-go rounds,
smiling faces, plastic horses spinning in slow motion.
On the helicopter ride, the playmakers pull the lever up,
then down,
stopping the machine while they work the crowd.

Will the politicians sight-see the border?
Examine, detect the face of the little girl?
I wonder where her roller-coaster ride will land her.
I feel the sluggish, steamy heat of summer,
I wonder what's happening,
the drudgery, time stopped, like a pendulum swaying
grandfather clock no longer working,
or the flow of water supply in summer's drought,
draining to a trickle
at the outlet of the Gulf of Mexico.

But wait!
A neighborhood swimming pool—where I live—
not a contaminated, public slush pile
of blamers and shamers (I call them)
harbors a dream where I, in community, learned to dive
deep off the board.

When I heard that the low-frequency sounds
of whale
travel more than 10,000 miles,
I took hope.
I think, the little girl floating in June,
hears an eerie voice, perhaps an adult calling her name.
The little girl creates a haunting melody,
her voice carrying like the whale song.
With two-way communication mated,
the little girl—a splash-born dreamer—hears
coming down our road
the Good Humor Man ice cream trucks.

In my suburb, I hear the jingle,
the liberty bell of independent operators calling
themselves Vintage
Ice Cream Guys. Popular from Florida to New York,
these guys stop in neighborhoods like mine,
freezing ice cream on a stick.
These ice cream guys, a "comeback," older adults say.

Thousands of miles away, the little girl,
I think, comes back or goes to a neighborhood
where whole milk creams—like a child dreams—
a place where the kind operators, the drivers, tip their hats.

The long-awaited line up.
Children run into the streets.
They stop to taste
their first, strawberry delight—
leaving behind—
the curried blood
of their fatherland.

Acknowledgements

The Avalon Literary Review, "The Unfettered Life"

The Broadkill Review, "Front Porch Sitting"

Broomweed Journal, "Sacred Land"

ByLine Magazine, "Page Torn from Tea Leaves"

Cathexis Northwest Press, "In the Spirit of Emily Dickinson"

The Closed Eye Open, "Slate Blue"

Eclectica, "First Bells"

The MacGuffin, "Winter Breath"

Miller's Pond, "Solitude" and reprint of "Page Torn from Tea Leaves"

Pegasus, "Citrus Delight"

Plants & Poetry Journal, "Nameless Tumbleweeds" and "Poetry Veins"

Poetry Quarterly, "Hope seals the virus" and "Turn Signals"

Querencia Press, "Full Moon"

Snapdragon, reprint of "November Cloak"

Tiny Seed Literary Journal, "The Great Monarch Migration"

Wild Roof Journal, "Talking Trees," "Where a Turtle Leads," and "The Bridge"

The Write Launch, "Between Being and Doing," "November Cloak," "Back to the Roots," "Sunrise," "When fear rises," and "A Forecast of Severe Storms Today"

Printed in the USA
CPSIA information can be obtained
at www.ICGtesting.com
CBHW021946230824
13639CB00004B/110